T0029957

All That Happiness Is

Also by Adam Gopnik

Through the Children's Gate: A Home in
New York

The King in the Window

Paris to the Moon

Americans in Paris: A Literary Anthology

High & Low: Modern Art and Popular Culture
(with Kirk Varnedoe)

Musical Theater

Our Table (with David Shire)

Fairy Tale (with Andrew Lippa)

Sentences (with Nico Muhly)

All That Happiness Is

Some Words on What Matters

Adam Gopnik

Liveright Publishing Corporation

A Division of W. W. Norton & Company
Independent Publishers Since 1923

For information about permission to reproduce selections from this
book, write to Permissions, Liveright Publishing Corporation,
a division of W. W. Norton & Company, Inc.,
500 Fifth Avenue, New York, NY 10110

For information about special discounts for bulk purchases, please
contact W. W. Norton Special Sales at specialsales@wwnorton.com or
800-233-4830

Manufacturing by Versa Press
Production manager: Anna Oler
Cover design by Steve Attardo

ISBN 978-1-324-09485-2

Liveright Publishing Corporation
500 Fifth Avenue, New York, N.Y. 10110
www.wwnorton.com

W. W. Norton & Company Ltd.
15 Carlisle Street, London W1D 3BS

1 2 3 4 5 6 7 8 9 0

For Ruthie & Richard Rogers.
Who taught us how to share it.

All That Happiness Is

What is happiness? And where can you find it, if you ever can? We all know that its pursuit is guaranteed, right there in the Declaration of Independence—sort of improbably; I don't think many political charters include such a lighthearted instruction, the phrase "the pursuit of happiness" suggesting picnics and fireworks and flirtation more than it suggests the stern work of revolution.

Still it's a phrase we love, even if it still does seem to attach lesser individual ambition to a nobler and more collective countrywide one—as if someone would write today, in a charter of freedoms, that we have inalienable rights to life, liberty, and steadier reception on all streaming services. It's the kind of thing that it would be *nice* to have or pursue, though perhaps not quite the first thing you would want to *announce* you wanted to have. We'd keep it quiet until after the revolution was won.

Yet there it is, even if the phrase, as a historian of philosophy would tell you—as one not long ago told me—has been amputated from its source, guaranteeing only the *pursuit* of happiness and not its capture. The seventeenth-century English philosopher John Locke, who originated the term, meant by it both the pursuit *and* the capture and, probably, a better afterlife in heaven as well.

But the "mere" American pursuit of happiness, however plaintively isolated from its intellectual origins, has its odd charm, made familiar by time. We all seek happiness, or seem to, and there is no end of books to offer us recipes, or drugs, to induce the state artificially. Is happiness sensual pleasure? Seems too superficial. Spiritual pursuit? Seems too unreal. A good meal? A great bottle? The success of our causes? All seem either too narrowly material or else too piously impractical. A cause well won leads to another cause, and a bottle well drunk is empty.

Mystics, if you meet one, will tell you that the search is wrongheaded, and that we search not to be happy but to not *need* to be happy. It is wise but perhaps unduly discouraging counsel. Yet we are perhaps closer to our experience, and to those mystics, if we locate happiness not in something gained but in something lost—the loss of ourselves in something "other." Most people who have found some moment of happiness in life point to a moment when this happened, when they lost themselves to find themselves.

Here's mine. When I was twelve, I disappeared into my bedroom with a $40 folk guitar and a giant book of Beatles songs, with elementary large-type "E-Z" chord diagrams to follow. I had no musical "gift," as a series of failed piano lessons had assured me—the teachers who gave the lessons had assured me, I mean; the lessons were merely dull—and no musical training. My fingers stung as I tried to press down on the strings without making them buzz, and my left hand ached as I tried—and for a long time failed—stretching it across the neck. Nonetheless, I worked my way through "Rain" (two chords) and then "Love Me Do" (three) and finally "Yellow Submarine" (four, or was it five?) and discovered by myself the matchless thrill of homemade musical harmony.

I can still recall the days I spent with those chords. The arbitrary match of these hand gymnastics with the most powerful emotions I had so far felt in life was astounding to me. The ringing beauty of the G chord, for instance, which, awkwardly strung out across the six strings of the whole neck—so that the little finger had to take up precarious and painful residence on the third fret of the highest string while the first fingers sat with difficulty on the two lowest ones, a world away—completely "paid off" for the pain by leaving the three middle strings open to what musicians call "sympathetic resonance." That the G chord sounds so pleasing only on guitar is in itself significant; songs written in G are very often guitar-based, just as ones in the equally "tactile" piano key of E flat are most often written there, E flat being a key you can play on guitar only with some semi-expert barring.

Trained musicians, transcribing Beatles songs onto paper, dutifully put the more harmonically "sophisticated" G6 chords in as "passing" chords. The reason is that John Lennon would simply lift his fingers from the fretboard in between chords and strum the open strings, which happen—as he wouldn't have known—to make that chord. I, too, played by lifting fingers and wrote a song that, I realize now, depended on the play of an open-sixth chord and a suspended major chord made with two fingers—I had no idea that this was what they might be called, or what I might have been doing—but I had more fun and a more audacious sense of harmony than I do now when I know the names and reasons. Nor did I know that two of the most inventive of songwriters of that moment, Joni Mitchell and Keith Richards, were both playing at the same time creatively with the "open tunings" I stumbled on by mistake—Joni because an early attack of polio had left her with a hand weakened in making bar chords, Keith because of a hand weakened in making bar chords by causes more immediately proximate than childhood polio.

Then, how astonishing it was to discover that the crude arithmetic of the chords—choose one note, then count three up, then count to five and then play all three notes at once—produced complicated emotions. By this simplest of rules, the second and third chords in the scale were both inevitably minor, while the fourth was major, which hit me with a thunderstruck emotion that I can still remember, that I can still *feel*, not least because the rising, poignant chord patterns of "Blackbird" and "Here, There and Everywhere" were *right there*, under my control, produced by fingers roaming through a preordained system, like an ant climbing up the Eiffel Tower—the iron girders immutable, but the direction the ant goes chosen by the ant.

I could have learned all of this in music theory class, but it would not have had a tenth the power. I had entered a dream labyrinth—no, not a dream, because the whole point was that it was *work*, manual labor—but where, by making shapes, signs, with your hands, you stumbled on primal scenes, familiar songs, beautiful sounds, one after another.

No one asked me to do this—no one wanted it, and doubtless those in my life weren't sorry the door was closed as I stumbled along after music. But the sense of happiness I felt that week remains resonant, if not always cheaply available to me, to this day. Fifty years later, I am not a much better guitar player now than I was then, but that week's work, and the months and years of self-directed practice on the instrument that followed it, became a touchstone of sorts for me, and a foundation for almost every meaningful thing I've done in my life since.

My own account of guitar chords learned, and life begun, seems to echo in the experience of so many other people. A woman I know recalls learning to sew her own clothes by the same process I undertook—breaking it down into small, manageable tasks, getting the pattern, choosing the fabric, working the machine, until you found yourself making another kind of harmony, in this case wearing that beautiful thing you've made. The experience of breaking down and building up she learned then informed her later professional work as a film editor and producer. The Scottish poet and aphorist Don Paterson tells rapturously in his memoir of a working-class boyhood of becoming improbably obsessed with Japanese origami. "I remember turning a page of an origami guide, to find a photo of an origami elephant. I was speechless. It was less an elephant than an essay on elephantness, a distillation of all that ever was or would be elephant; it was the form that threw its shadow on the cave. . . . I spent the next two and a half years of my life doing nothing but origami from dawn to dusk which—a recurrent theme—began to worry my parents." (So forlorn was his search for origami partners in Dundee that Paterson eventually appeared in the local newspaper under the headline: "Donald Is Seeking Fellow Paper Folders.")

Sometimes, a new passion can shade into an eventual vocation. I read, in that year when

I started strumming purposefully, the inspiring story of the young Beatles themselves going across town, on a Liverpool bus, to meet a guy who knew a B dominant seventh chord, a vital link in the key of E. It is on the surface so ridiculous a pursuit that its truth has been doubted—if you know an A7, you ought to see how a B7 gets made!—but it is, doubtless, true. Paul McCartney has confirmed it many times.

Guitar players generally found places to play with other guitar players, though the need for the place where they played to be sufficiently shielded from pained listeners gave a name to a whole genre, the garage band. Yet obsessive, seemingly unproductive adolescent love for an art form can provoke big stuff: Dickens in *David Copperfield* remembers the same kind of adolescent escape in the act of reading novels and becoming Tom Jones as a flight from the indignities of his Micawberish upbringing. Closer to home, another friend recalls struggling to draw *anything* as a kid—Superman, Spider-Man—and being astonished by his own growing skill as each week one more piece of the world got decrypted on paper. He became a realist painter.

But most often these early self-directed obsessions produce not a job to earn from but a platform to leap from—a sense of fulfillment through passionate perseverance that crosses over into the most seemingly alien enterprises. They were not self-advantaging achievements; they were self-emancipating accomplishments.

For that is the first truth about what happiness is that seems sound, almost self-evident—that genuine happiness is always rooted in absorption in something outside us, and begins in accomplishment undertaken for its own sake and pursued to its own odd and buzzing ends. A set of stumbling dance steps, a cascade of blows choreographed by a boxing coach, a pattern of chords imprinted on a lead sheet suddenly cease to be the difficult, hard-to-memorize, isolated awkwardnesses that they have been for weeks or months, and come together in a way that—however inadequate to the watching eye or listening ear of expertise—feels, for the one undertaking it, like something as new as it is blissful. Through sheer perseverance, motivated by some passion for the pursuit that might seem at times perverse in its persistence, the steps have turned into a seamless, or at least seemingly seamless, sequence. The pursuer is rarely aware that this is happening as it happens and knows it less through consciously knowing it than through the onset of happiness it mysteriously produces—the awareness, which may follow on the action by mere microseconds, that what began as something conscious and effortful now just *is*.

In the psychological literature—particularly in the pop-psychological literature—this apparition is called simply "the flow." We intuitively know that it references a state not of self-possession but of rapturous self-*loss*. It is perhaps the strongest cognitive opiate human beings produce. The flow may be a term, like "the Force" in the Star Wars saga, that seems suspiciously squishy. (Is a student ecstatically finishing a paper at three a.m. actually in the flow or merely under the gun?) But that it exists in some form or another no one doubts. There are many opiates available to inject into our veins; this is the only one that we produce ourselves and self-inject into our brains.

I think of this state simply as that of accomplishment. By *accomplishment* I mean the engulfing activity we've chosen, whose reward is the rush of fulfilment, the sense of happiness that rises uniquely from absorption in a thing outside ourselves. It stands in contrast to the more familiar, more legible *achievement*, which I would define as the completion of a task imposed from outside—the reward often being a path to the next achievement.

Our social world conspires to denigrate these accomplishments in favor of the rote work of achievement. All our observation tells us that kids, in particular, are perpetually being pushed toward the next test, toward the "best" college they can get into. We invent achievement tests designed to be completely immune to coaching, and therefore we have ever more expensive coaches to break the code of the non-coachable achievement test. (Those who can't afford such absurdities are simply left out.) Kids and young adults are driven toward achievement, meaning tasks that lead only to other tasks, resembling not so much a rat race as a rat maze, with another hit of sugar water waiting around the bend, but the path to the center—or the point of it all—never made plain.

What typically emerges from looking at young people, gifted and ordinary, is that, from their own points of view, *accomplishment* counts for far more in their inner lives than does achievement—the competition won, the reward secured. The unexpected pleasures of accomplishment, felt in your mind or muscles, is more compelling than the concreteness of achievement, the trophy pressed in your hands. What sustains us in any competition are the moments of interiority when the competition vanishes; what sustains us in any struggle are the moments when we forget the struggle. Philippe Petit didn't walk the wire between the Twin Towers by working harder while he was up there; he worked hard to get to a state where being up there would never feel like work.

As a parent, I've seen the pure satisfaction of accomplishment, of a particular passion arduously pursued, arise in my own children. Yet I've also seen it actively discouraged by the well-meaning schools they attended: My son Luke, who was, at twelve, a boy enchanted by Dai Vernon's card tricks, a pack forever in his hands, found that the many hours he's spent learning the Erdnase color-change is not a necessarily rewarded act in eighth grade. I fought a good fight on his behalf to cut down on homework—a fight that landed eventually on the front page of the *New York Times*, exactly because homework was, in plain English, cutting into his magic. I may have been naïve, but I was, surely, not wholly wrong; the steps he has taken in life that led him eventually to pursue graduate degrees in philosophy began there. The concentration and subtlety of mind required to master Wittgenstein's parables can be rooted more readily in the art of "twisting the aces" than in getting A's. Self-directed accomplishment, no matter how absurd it may look to outsiders or how partial it may be, can become a foundation of our sense of self, and of our sense of possibility. Losing ourselves in an all-absorbing action, we become ourselves.

The issue, in a way, goes deeper than questions of how best to use our mental energies. It speaks to everything we want out of life. If we make life subject to a rule of achievement— does it pay? Does it work?—we not only betray our values but we make a joke of our time on Earth. Because in the long run, *nothing* is going to work out.

I like to call this the Causal Catastrophe: the belief that the proof of the rightness or wrongness of some way of proceeding in life is the ultimate result. This appears, on the surface, so uncontroversial a position—what other standard would you use except the long-term consequences?— that to question it seems a little odd. But chains of human causality are, if not infinite, very long; in every life, *some* bad consequence of your upbringing will eventually emerge.

We disapprove, for instance, of parental hovering not because it won't pay off later—it might; it does!—but because it's obnoxious now. Strenuously competitive parents may indeed produce high-achieving grown-ups, but it's in the nature of things that high-achieving adults are likely to become frustrated and embittered old people once the rug is pulled out from under their ambition. If a chain is only as strong as its weakest link, then all chains are weak, since everybody ends up broken.

I've talked about the difference between achievement and accomplishment many times, and I'm aware of at least some of the objections to this view. At some moment, the impatient insist, all accomplishment, however self-directed, has to become professional, lucrative, real. We can't play with cards, or chords, forever. And surely many of the things that we are asked to achieve can lead to self-discovery; taught well, we may learn to love new and unexpected things for their own sake. The trick may lie in the teaching. My sister, Alison Gopnik, a leading developmental psychologist, puts this well: if we taught kids softball the way we teach them science, they would hate softball as much as they hate science; but if we taught them science as we teach them softball, by practice and absorption, they might love both.

The moment when a particular accomplishment we've pursued suddenly becomes the pattern of a possible life is as large a moment as that first private moment, that bedroom moment, when the accomplishment first winks its eye and beckons us along. Ambition is a good thing, especially if it is the catalyst that lets an accomplishment become a vocation. We have to make a living doing something, and one of the worst things that happens to us is making a living doing work we don't like. Focused work, the drive to prevail, the acquirement of persistence against procrastination that everyone is subject to—these are positive traits, at least in the world we've made for ourselves.

But there are different kinds of ambition. There is ambition to accomplish something; and there is ambition merely to prevail over others. For highly competitive people, learning the difference can be a lifetime's work. I hardly offer my own life as a tracery of anything too exceptional—if anything, it is the typical nature of the path I found, how well-worn it is by others, that strikes me—but after that epiphany with the guitar at twelve, the next most important event in my own inner development occurred around age twenty-two, when I discovered that my ambition to be a writer could only be *achieved* if I made the mental work of writing into the sheer physical work of writing.

Writing might be an imaginative act in the end, but it is an athletic act when you begin. You had to sit there, treating the typewriter—as it would still remain for another few years—as though it were a stationary bike, just there to be ridden, for a set number of hours. You don't ride it well or badly; you just ride it. Your brain, you learn, is smarter than your mind, and the simple act of harvesting words, producing three pages or three thousand words each day, indifferent to their quality until afterward—so that you also learn that while something bad can always be made better, something that doesn't exist can't be made into anything at all—becomes the open door to a life of work. Learning to work hard is as important as learning to work well. Accomplishment becomes a place to live only when it is graced—and that is the right word—by ambition.

Yet another objection to my plea against the tyranny of achievement is simply that "accomplishment" is just the name people of good fortune give to things that they have the "privilege" of doing, which achievement has already put them in a place to pursue. Accomplishment is merely the rich kids' name for free time. It fills hours that their parents' and their grandparents' and their great-grandparents' purpose (or, privilege, they're often hard to distinguish) have bequeathed to them.

In truth, accomplishment is the most genuinely *egalitarian* aspect of human enterprise. Being good at things is an artisanal more than an aristocratic business. Every enterprise, every job, every short-order recipe—everything we do can be done more or less beautifully, and everyone knows it. (One of the few reliable questions any reporter can ask of any subject is simply "Who's the best you know in what you do? Who's the Wayne Gretzky of . . ." and it can be plumbing or painting, but there's an instant answer. "Oh, Joe Calisano!" the lesser plumber answers at once. "That guy is such a genius with a wrench in his hand that he can turn the water on and off in a whole city with a flick of his wrist.") Accomplishment provides its pleasures, historically, to classes otherwise marginalized or patronized. To belittle it is to accept, unconsciously, exactly the distinction between major and minor, significant and insignificant, that social coercion—what we used

to call, quaintly but not wrongly, "the system"—
has always been there to perpetuate. We too
often denigrate the smaller artisanal triumphs of
bread-baking and batik-making as mere women's
work—a denigration not made more dignified by
being given a pseudo-progressive slant.

The complaints about "accomplishment" hardly seem fatal, especially against the sometimes-secret rewards the practice of accomplishment offers. Those rewards are so evident that, to borrow the title of a Feydeau farce, they have a name for it in France. I was chopping onions once while working on a story, the most aged of *stages*, unpaid assistants, in a three-star Paris kitchen, when one of the hardened pro chefs peeked over my shoulder and condescending to my chopping with a single raised eyebrow, in his best French self-cartooning fashion, said, as I understood him: "You're an author, Mr. Gopnik? Ah. So cooking is your Ingres Violin." It was one of those expressions in a foreign tongue when we grasp the words, hear the vocabulary—and can't quite credit that what was said was said. *I think he said that the onions I was chopping were like a violin belonging to Ingres.* I must have misheard him. Or maybe it was an elegant insult, a thing not unknown in France. Or maybe what I heard as "Ingres" was one of those skmooshed-together subject-verb phrases that trick your ear.

But, home that night, checking it quietly online, I realized that what he had said was what he had said. Though countless French idioms have worked their way into English, from *fait accompli* to *tour de force*, the *violon d'Ingres* is one that hasn't. It references Jean-Auguste Dominique Ingres, the great nineteenth-century

French neoclassical painter, a hypersensitive master of exquisitely detailed, maniacally meticulous portraits—who had a secondary passion, equally intense if not equally unique, for playing the violin.

And then I knew that what the chef said was what he had said . . . and that what he had said was true: cooking, usually at home, not under expert eyes, is my secondary passion, the one that fuels all others. Chopping onions is my entry to happiness. Though Ingres never graduated beyond playing second violin in a provincial orchestra, he donated his prized instrument to the same museum to which he also left all his grander art. He wanted violin and paintbrush to have equal weight in his legacy. We translate the French idiom very misleadingly as a "hobby"—but the violin wasn't a hobby for Ingres at all. It was a parallel passion, and it fed the already fully achieved virtuosic technical level of his primary art.

In France, it's an immediately lucid metaphor. A few decades ago, the *pâtissier* Christian Constant opened a restaurant called Le Violon d'Ingres exactly to play on it: he made croissants, but he dreamt of cream sauces. This isn't unusual. Einstein, too, had his violin, as Chaplin had his, and doubtless the greatest violinists tend to have their own secret labs or baggy pants. The so-called secondary accomplishment, in its incompleteness, gave them, as it may give us, better access to the state that was the reason that they first pursued the primary one. We use a paintbrush better for playing the violin worse.

The feeling of accomplishment, and our search for it—our attempt to *capture* it—is subject to another truth, close to a paradox, of the chopping-onions kind. It is that accomplishment is more available to amateur experience than to even expert professional work. As we mature, we find this sensation—whatever we want to call it—more potently in our secondary passions than in our primary purposes. When we pursue the flow, we find, again and again, that we are really playing Ingres's violin.

So many of us, as I've said, first experience that rush of feeling as adolescents, when we fall into something where the rewards of inner satisfaction seem so extreme that they become a near addiction. Yet as we professionalize and "vocationalize" it, that first rapture becomes less rapt. It is good to say "follow your bliss," as graduation speeches tend to do. But as life moves forward, we soon become acutely aware of the space between the scale of our ambitions and the completeness of our accomplishments. Accomplishment is a self-diminishing cycle. The better we become at something, the less pleasure it supplies inside. I once wrote a profile of a winemaker who makes terrific California Grenache and Syrah . . . and remains perpetually disappointed with his own bottlings, because he had as the standard within his head and sense-memory the greatest years of Château Rayas and the like. Nothing was ever going to rise to that level. He could only experience the distance between his original ambitions and his—to his eye, or nose—inadequate accomplishment.

Similarly, a writer who after decades writing certainly knows something about the art, still starts each sentence with the hope that what's coming will be as forthright as Jane Austen, as rhapsodically sensual as John Updike, as intricately ruminative as Proust . . . and ends each day having written only more of his own sentences. The guys and girls who summit Everest in the jauntiest spirit feel accomplishment, surely— but know better all the crevasses they mis-stepped along the way.

As these examples do suggest, though the *feeling* of accomplishment may be remarkably similar from place to place and accomplishment to accomplishment, its realization is necessarily compound. It's not just made up of a sudden swoon of self-release; it's a self-release that's self-disciplined and bounded by countless specific features. The specificities of the experience are what gives it character and makes it live for us in memory.

It's not just that we learn guitar chords—it's guitar chords at age twelve in a room with a shut door and a Beatles record playing in another room beyond. It's Japanese origami pursued in a working-class neighborhood in Scotland. It's card magic reinvigorated by regular trips to a magic shop across from the Empire State Building. It's all the reasons why human psychology will never be fully explained or pictured by scientific investigation—there are just too many variables, too many vectors pressing on every incident. It's the reason why storytelling and songwriting and poetry-making will always be so much more effective organizers and vehicles of our experience than studies in social science. They alone convey it accurately in all its infrangible many-sidedness. A song, as the great songwriter Yip Harburg said once, is the only form that gives us an idea *and* the emotion provoked by that idea, not in sequence but at the same time. Proust's famous point about the madeleine and memory was not that small French pastries unlock forgotten moments; it's that our experience is so multiply and individually encoded that the most easily overlooked element might be the one that turns out to be the key to deciphering its hieroglyphs. It's not the madeleine that gets dipped into the tea that matters; it's the whole damned cup of tea and the room it gets poured in.

At the same time, accomplishment is bounded by the eternal truths of repetition and habituation and exhaustion and renewal. We get better at guitar chords, and so playing that open G stops giving us the same pleasure. We have to make a bar chord or learn, laboriously, a G-minor ninth . . . or simply pass beyond chord-finding to the mysteries of song-making, which inevitably start up under our fingers too. (I wrote forty or so songs by the time I was twenty, as the chords turned themselves into tunes that I had not sought but found.) We need another stimulus, a new preoccupation, a new drug as the song says—even if it's the same drug, the cognitive opiate of avidity and accomplishment, in a new form.

And so, it's exactly when we *don't* have access to any kind of perfection that happiness comes into view. It's in the dancing lessons we undertake at fifty, the fencing class we take at sixty, or simply in the Sunday painting our grandfather loved to do as well. These restore us to our adolescent condition of sheer absorption in a thing outside ourselves. That's one reason why people of enormous evident achievement tend not to be narrowly focused on the one thing they do but to be most passionately open to subsidiary or parallel pursuits.

Most important of all is the realization that our habit of patronizing or diminishing those whose search for the rush of accomplishment takes them to secondary pursuits, however modest—from watercolor painting to yoga class—is a tremendous mistake. "No one who's really using his ego has time for any hobbies," Salinger's Zooey Glass announces in sad summary in *Franny and Zooey*. But one wonders if it isn't wiser to say, as Seymour Glass might have, that the hobbyist is someone who has, however momentarily, surmounted her ego in pursuit of her true self. The one force we can rely on in life is the force of learning new things as we get older, and as we age. Too often condescended to, it seems like one sure thing worth celebrating.

Playing the music of our secondary selves, we discover the sound of our souls. Resonating to it, we find ourselves renewed. I play my Ingres violin as best I can. Every morning at nine, I make new sentences. Every night at six, I chop new onions. The beautiful paradox is that pursuing things we may at first do poorly can produce the sense of absorption, which *is* all that happiness is, while persisting in those we already do well does not. The retired woman, easily dismissed, who is taking that course in life drawing has rocket fuel in her hands.

The most serious objection made to the celebration of accomplishment is that, by focusing too exclusively on pleasure, on "self-realization," we escape too quickly from the necessary public sphere of duty and citizenship into a merely private realm of narcissistic fulfillment. We are finding chords and playing with cards and plucking our secondary violin while blind to our neighbors. They are burning while we fiddle.

Yet there's a reason—instinctive in their time but ever more widely understood today— why Jefferson and the rest insisted on the pursuit of happiness in their hopeful catalogue of revolutionary purpose. For it is exactly both the test and the foundation of a healthy society that it encourages the pursuit of private pleasures and encourages their mutual tolerance. By far the most important conception of a "liberal" society—in the sense of a society committed to argument, elections, and the oscillation of power—is not democracy or equality alone. It is pluralism. Pluralism in politics and political parties, sure, but a pluralism that extends so deeply in our imaginations and practices that it rests in the end on a pluralism of pleasures.

A pluralist politics *must* rest on a pluralism of pleasures. That's the lesson of every serious inquiry into the foundations of democracy— whether experiential and firsthand or "scientific" and statistical—of the past hundred years. Some of these pleasures are the obvious ones of close family and warm friends, though even these relationships depend on the protection of privacy, in a way that is rarely accessible in authoritarian societies. The French revolutionaries who came after the American ones emphasized the primacy of the private realm in a free society. If we can't draw a line between the private and the public, then everyone's conduct becomes everyone's business, and we are "on view" all day and night in ways that no idea of happiness can sustain. We want time in our bedrooms to do what we want, whether chord-hunting or making other kinds of music.

But healthy societies also have a variety and abundance of pursued *public* pleasures. They're the kind made in compact with others, and usually crossing lines of caste and creed. You could pick out the Italian towns most likely to become functionally democratic by the number of amateur opera societies each contained. You could predict which developing countries would tolerate democracy by how well they danced. The "velvet revolutions" of the '70s were all rooted in civil society more than in civic rules.

The Enlightenment itself began not with isolated philosophes making pronouncements but in coffeehouse conversations, and the quality of the coffee and the exaltations of the talk were one. A set of pointless-seeming, drifting "accomplishments" accomplished the big change. We become better citizens when we become musicians, because musicians play in bands and magicians can only work in clubs. A tuba player is of necessity a citizen of the orchestra. Mutual pleasure teaches us mutual reliance. We take up playing softball—or even just take up watching baseball—and we learn citizenship by turning double-plays and stealing home, or simply by sitting in the stands and cheering on someone else to do it. (My identity as a Quebecker relies entirely on my role as a fan of the Montreal Canadiens, a community-crossing affiliation.)

A pluralistic society allows us to play *with* our pleasures, in every sense—to decide that we want to play ragas instead of rock music, or to turn ragas into a form of rock music—and is the only kind of society that has a ground, a foundation, a set of practices, that respects other people's pleasures. Without "civil society," without conversations not in themselves overtly political but drawn from reservoirs of social trust and protected by liberal institutions, no laws or rules can help. Without experience in working alongside those not of our clan or kind in non-political pursuits, we can't practice politics in a persuasively pluralistic way. That seemingly incongruous practice of fireworks and flirtations—exactly the pursuit of happiness promised in the Declaration—is not only what makes freedom worthwhile. It is, all the evidence of study and our own experience suggests, what makes free cities free.

Every day of my working life, I walk ten thousand steps in or bike once around Central Park, and it turns me back to one of my personal heroes, Frederick Law Olmsted, who designed it, and to the lesson that the park he conceived was not meant to be a sylvan escape from the pressures of urban life. It was meant to be exactly the antidote to the virus of a nightmarish, immobile, stagnant society of the kind he had experienced as a journalist reporting on the slave states of the American South—before he envisioned so much as a square inch of park land, when he saw that the slave states were not only a cruel society but a paralyzed one.

Olmsted compared the fixed, limited, feudal, "vertical" society he found in the South with the open, "horizontal" one he had left in the North. In a memorable, Whitmanesque passage he wrote that the young people of the North were: "members and managers of reading rooms, public libraries, gymnasiums, game clubs, boat clubs, ball clubs, and all sorts of clubs, Bible classes, debating societies, military companies; they are planting road-side trees, or damming streams for skating ponds, or rigging diving-boards, or getting up fireworks displays, or private theatricals; they are always doing something." Central Park exists to be a kind of canvas on which we can paint our own pictures, an apparatus for our own accomplishment.

And the more confidently we pursue our own accomplishments, the less time we have to hate and fear other people's. The rise of autocracy in America is much less the consequence of a part of the population insisting on pursuing its own vision of the good life than on one part hating with a passion the vision of the good life that others pursue, until the hatred becomes the only pleasure. The only accomplishment left is preventing someone else from having theirs.

Now, I don't want to turn a universal human truth into a narrower liberal-democratic one. Obviously, countless commoners in a monarchy, or for that matter gondoliers under the damp Venetian oligarchy, pursued accomplishment. The lens-maker in the Renaissance, like Galileo, or the lute player in a ducal court, like his father . . . or the sonnet-maker in an Elizabethan one, felt all the same emotions of secret satisfaction and inner realization that we do. (Just read Shakespeare's own sonnets to experience, at a remove, the internal press of phrase-making and the self-delight in pulling it off.) Accomplishment is not peculiar to liberal democracies, or to modern people.

But when we think of Shakespeare or Galileo or Emily Dickinson, we recognize that they lived in societies that, however remote their political values might be, made space for individual pursuits, even if that space was narrower than the kinds we might want. They got to find their accomplishments among like-minded people, sometimes among extremely competitive like-minded people. (Galileo learned the danger of "leaping spaces" in an authoritarian society, so to speak, when the Church told him to shut up or be tortured.) Accomplishment depends on the existence of a community where it can implant itself and grow. Historically, we've moved in the direction of broadening the foundation of our world to open it up to more talents. The more open a society is, the more space there is for accomplishment.

It's usually said, on the social-scientific side of the study, that what matters most to human happiness is the strength of our connections to family and friends. Who can deny their value? Yet perhaps, the more particular, not to say perverse, eye of the humanist—or at least of the humorist—suggests that happiness moves in a more spiraling, circular movement than that static picture suggests. Pretty much all dramatic literature exists to remind us that happy families are not always so, or not so for long, and that friends, as *Friends* failed to explore, tend to drift away insensibly as much as they magnetize to us for life. In the genuinely shifting field of ties, weak and strong, permanent and portable, illicit and official, it's the things we're good at that tend to amplify and aerate our connections. In plain English, accomplishment is attractive. It takes place in circles of engagement and yes, of course, of rewards. First you play for your (bored but attentive) parents; then for your (competitive) friends; and at last, onstage for (a more-or-less engaged, depending on the state of their blood stream) audience. Accomplishment is an adhesive and an expander. Our circles of self-making expand as we escape ourselves. Doubtless we do find our happiness most often with a circle of friends or family around a dinner table. But the circle expands as our lives expand, and that's a good thing. It's not an accident that when we talk about what someone does particularly well, we talk about what they alone "bring to the table." We love our family, mostly, and we care for our friends, when we can, but the one thing we all tend not to love is freeloaders. As Olmsted said, we like people who do things. Private affections activate accomplishments, and accomplishments in turn broaden our affective ties. It's a happy kind of circle.

And so, one of the keenest reproaches we can make to the way we live now is that we have amputated the social space that allows *this* social flow to happen. When we look around America, or at many countries in Europe, not to mention the rest of the world, we see depredation that robs people of the time or place to find and make their way. A sense of community and self-worth is degraded and music-making, literally, gets harder.

There are many places in the world that used to have communities where now there are none. The Beatles were poor kids, but they grew up, in pre-Thatcher Britain, in a coherent city with church fetes to find a partner at and music stores to find a manager in. Another rock star, Chrissie Hynde, writes beautifully about how coherent the Akron, Ohio, she grew up in was, with rock clubs and underground magazine stores. Accomplishment is private in the first instance, but it's social in the second instance, and worse even than being economically desperate is being culturally desperate, having no meaningful sense of community and continuity.

And so, if we want the pleasure of individual accomplishment, we can't allow large swathes of it to be gutted. Accomplishment and community are a circle. My parents were graduate students, children of immigrants, and far from wealthy or "privileged." But they could afford a little house in a university neighborhood. I had a bedroom, shared with my brother, and a guitar, shared with my sister. It wasn't much, but it wasn't nothing. It was enough for accomplishment—and happiness—to be possible. One thing we should all work for is for everyone today, of every background and creed and political persuasion, to have the same.

Constant happiness is perhaps unachievable, or achievable only in bursts and bits—the fatality of life is inescapable, and our dissolutions and deaths never pretty. And yet within that span, if we are lucky enough to avoid the more vivid forms of persecution and oppression, bursts of delight do arise, regularly, compounded of exhilaration, meaning, poignant pleasure, often sharp-edged desire. We seem to pursue those best by pursuing them indirectly, just the way we woo our loves. The first thing every boy learns in the art of impressing women is that if a woman is listening to you at all, she's as impressed as she's ever going to be. What matters is making meaning. Everything else is the human comedy, which we struggle merely to make humane.

Our accomplishments mark the sum of our happiness experienced—and that is the one kind of achievement worth achieving. The pursuit *is* the happiness. The tyranny of outer achievement will always be part of our world because ambition thrives permanently in our hearts and souls. What we can do is to make space, every day, for the sheer pleasure of learning new things—for even when we pursue accomplishments selfishly, they somehow help remake our selves. (Sex is the perfect example of a selfish action that involves the loss of one's self in another. It's a shared accomplishment, in every sense.)

Other people often teach us what we think even after we've said it. When I was on the road with a book about the search for mastery, many listeners and readers brought to me, with touching delicacy and excitement, a perfectly applicable poem by Rilke that I had been too ignorant to attach to my own investigations. It begins:

Whoever you may be: step into the evening. Step out
of the room where everything is known to you already . . .

All that happiness is. It is escape from the self into another, whether the "other" is a person, or a system, like a tonal system, that someone else, or many others, have left behind, like discarded snake skins, for us to slip into after.

Like so many people now, I love to contemplate the idea of the "multiverse" and the possibility that all that we have ever experienced somehow coexists in some unobtainable plane of simultaneity, with every time and age adjacent to every other. Somewhere, we imagine, at every moment, a girl is sewing patterns or singing songs and finding space for herself is at the same time, in a bend of time just beside, a woman making movies. A boy is working cards in front of a mirror at the same time that his older self is matching wits with Wittgenstein. We are all the things we have been and will be, all our moments spread out like a pack of cards expertly fanned across the universe.

And three boys on a Liverpool bus struggle with a B7 chord they have just learned, and the world begins anew. Are *they* happy? Well, we know that two have lost their mothers, and two will lose their own lives, tragically early . . . no future fame nor to-be-found latent genius can immunize them from the tragic truth of the world. But for now, yes, they are happy. We see their pleasure in their faces and sense it in their fingers. They have gone outside and made a world. They know a new chord.

About the Author

Adam Gopnik is a staff writer at *The New Yorker* and has written for the magazine since 1986. He has won three National Magazine Awards for essays and for criticism. The author of numerous best-selling books, including *Paris to the Moon*, he lives in New York City.